W9-ACR-537

Black Sabbath

Pioneers of Heavy Metal

Other Titles in REBELS OF ROCK

Library Ed. ISBN-13:
978-0-7660-3031-2
Paperback ISBN-13:
978-0-7660-3623-9

Library Ed. ISBN-13:
978-0-7660-3236-1
Paperback ISBN-13:
978-1-59845-210-5

Library Ed. ISBN-13:
978-0-7660-3379-5
Paperback ISBN-13:
978-1-59845-212-9

Library Ed. ISBN-13:
978-0-7660-3232-3
Paperback ISBN-13:
978-1-59845-211-2

Library Ed. ISBN-13:
978-0-7660-3234-7
Paperback ISBN-13:
978-1-59845-208-2

Library Ed. ISBN-13:
978-0-7660-3028-2
Paperback ISBN-13:
978-0-7660-3620-8

Library Ed. ISBN-13:
978-0-7660-3029-9
Paperback ISBN-13:
978-0-7660-3621-5

Library Ed. ISBN-13:
978-0-7660-3027-5
Paperback ISBN-13:
978-0-7660-3619-2

Library Ed. ISBN-13:
978-0-7660-3026-8
Paperback ISBN-13:
978-0-7660-3618-5

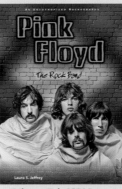

Library Ed. ISBN-13:
978-0-7660-3030-5
Paperback ISBN-13:
978-0-7660-3622-2

Library Ed. ISBN-13:
978-0-7660-3233-0
Paperback ISBN-13:
978-1-59845-213-6

Library Ed. ISBN-13:
978-0-7660-3231-6
Paperback ISBN-13:
978-1-59845-209-9

AN UNAUTHORIZED ROCKOGRAPHY

Black Sabbath

Pioneers of Heavy Metal

Brian Aberback

REBELS OF ROCK

 Enslow Publishers, Inc.
40 Industrial Road
Box 398
Berkeley Heights, NJ 07922
USA
http://www.enslow.com

Library of Congress Cataloging-in-Publication Data

Aberback, Brian.
    Black Sabbath : pioneers of heavy metal / Brian Aberback.
        p. cm. — (Rebels of rock)
    Includes bibliographical references and index.
    Summary: "A biography of British heavy metal band Black Sabbath"—Provided by publisher.
    ISBN 978-0-7660-3379-5
    1. Black Sabbath (Musical group)—Juvenile literature. 2. Rock musicians—England—
Biography—Juvenile literature. I. Title.
    ML3930.B578A34 2010
    782.42166092'2—dc22
    [B]   2009012295

ISBN-13: 978-1-59845-212-9 (paperback ed.)

Printed in the United States of America

052010 Lake Book Manufacturing, Inc., Melrose Park, IL

10 9 8 7 6 5 4 3 2 1

To Our Readers: This book has not been authorized by Black Sabbath or its successors.

We have done our best to make sure all Internet Addresses in this book were active and appropriate when we went to press. However, the author and the publisher have no control over and assume no liability for the material available on those Internet sites or on other Web sites they may link to. Any comments or suggestions can be sent by e-mail to comments@enslow.com or to the address on the back cover.

Every effort has been made to locate all copyright holders of material used in this book. If any errors or omissions have occurred, corrections will be made in future editions of this book.

♻ Enslow Publishers, Inc., is committed to printing our books on recycled paper. The paper in every book contains 10% to 30% post-consumer waste (PCW). The cover board on the outside of each book contains 100% PCW. Our goal is to do our part to help young people and the environment too!

Illustration Credits: Associated Press, pp. 6, 80, 84, 88; Andre Csillag/Rex USA/Courtesy Everett Collection, p. 59; Ian Dickson/Rex USA/Courtesy Everett Collection, p. 25; © Embassy Pictures/courtesy Everett Collection, p. 66; Everett Collection, pp. 34, 50, 72; LEG/Rex USA/ Courtesy Everett Collection, p. 17; Mary Evans Picture Library/Everett Collection, p. 28; © MTV/Courtesy Everett Collection, p. 74; Photofest, p. 62; © Pictorial Press Ltd/Alamy, p. 45; Brian Rasic/Rex USA, courtesy Everett Collection, p. 68; Redferns/Getty Images, p. 31; UPI Photo/Martin Fried/Landov, p. 87; Dick Wallis/Rex Features/Courtesy Everett Collection, pp. 12, 22; Chris Walter/Photofeatures.com, p. 65.

Cover Illustration: Associated Press.

CONTENTS

In 2006, Black Sabbath was inducted into the Rock and Roll Hall of Fame. From left to right: Ozzy Osbourne, Bill Ward, Tony Iommi, and Geezer Butler.

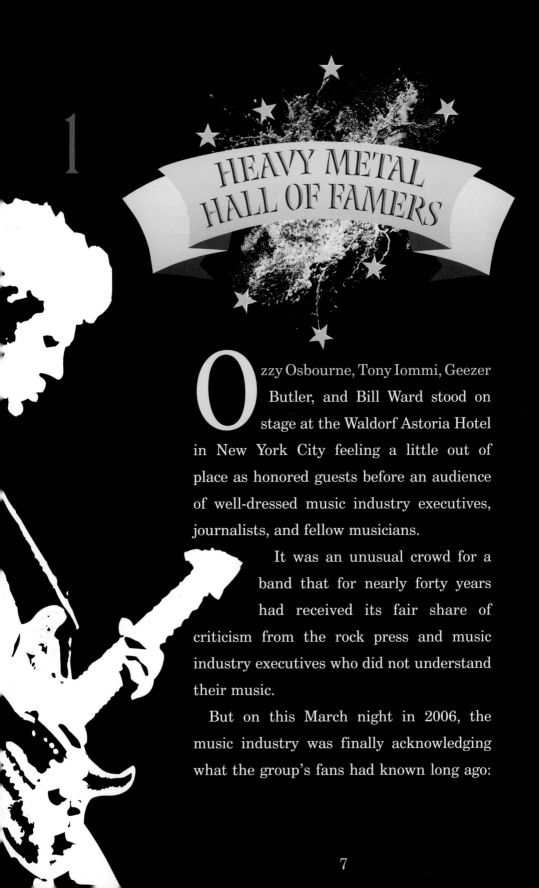

HEAVY METAL HALL OF FAMERS

O zzy Osbourne, Tony Iommi, Geezer Butler, and Bill Ward stood on stage at the Waldorf Astoria Hotel in New York City feeling a little out of place as honored guests before an audience of well-dressed music industry executives, journalists, and fellow musicians.

It was an unusual crowd for a band that for nearly forty years had received its fair share of criticism from the rock press and music industry executives who did not understand their music.

But on this March night in 2006, the music industry was finally acknowledging what the group's fans had known long ago:

Black Sabbath, the band that created heavy metal music, belonged in the Rock and Roll Hall of Fame.

Black Sabbath had previously been on the Hall of Fame ballot seven times, prompting Osbourne to ask that the voting committee permanently take the band off the ballot. Luckily for Black Sabbath, Osbourne's request was not granted.

During Black Sabbath's induction ceremony into the Hall of Fame that night, Ward told the crowd, "Hopefully, our induction tonight will add further validation . . . that hard rock and heavy metal may have an endearing and everlasting place in rock history."[1]

Black Sabbath could not envision making rock history when the band formed in Birmingham, England, in the late 1960s. Back then, the poor and working-class young men of Black Sabbath were hoping to simply make a living playing music so that they could escape a life confined to boring factory work.

The road to respectability had not been easy. Iommi noted, "In the Seventies nobody would mention Sabbath, nobody dared say they were into Sabbath, it was a dirty word to mention that you liked Sabbath. Nowadays, these bands are inspired by us and it's a good thing to do."[2]

The enormous impact that Black Sabbath has had on hard rock and heavy metal music was put into perspective by Metallica drummer Lars Ulrich, who, with bandmate James

Hetfield, gave the induction speeches for Black Sabbath at the Hall of Fame ceremony.

Ulrich, whose band is one of the biggest-selling rock acts in the world, said Black Sabbath's music was an essential influence on Metallica:

"If there was no Black Sabbath, there would be no Metallica. If there was no Black Sabbath, hard rock and heavy metal as we know it today would look, sound and be shaped very, very differently. . . . Black Sabbath is and always will be synonymous with the term 'heavy metal.'"[3]

The Hall of Fame induction was just one of several previously unlikely honors that Black Sabbath had recently received. The band won a Grammy Award in 2000 for a live version of the band's classic song, "Iron Man," and they performed their hit song, "Paranoid," at a special concert for Queen Elizabeth II in 2002.

Black Sabbath's journey from Birmingham to the big time is a remarkable story of highs and lows, of fallout and reconciliation. The rough road that the band members endured made their recognition as Rock and Roll Hall of Famers all the more satisfying. Iommi said, "I think we deserve to be in there more than most, and we should be in there. Without us, the music wouldn't be like it is today."[4]

MEET THE BAND

The original members of Black Sabbath were born within sixteen months of one another and grew up in Birmingham, England's second largest city. Birmingham was a major industrial center in the nineteenth and early twentieth centuries, defined by its foundries and factories that produced everything from heavy machinery and automobile parts to household utensils.

Though the members of Black Sabbath all were raised in the Aston section of Birmingham, they were not close friends as children. However, they shared a common experience growing up in poor and working-class families that would lead to a shared vision when they formed a band together as young men.

Ozzy Osbourne

John Michael Osbourne was born on December 3, 1948, the son of John Thomas and Lilian Osbourne. Osbourne was the fourth of six children and the first boy. He has two younger brothers, Paul and Tony, and three older sisters, Jean, Iris, and Gillian.

Osbourne grew up in a poor family. His father was a toolmaker and his mother worked in a factory that made automobile horns. The family lived in a cramped row house with only three rooms to house everyone.

The poorest member of Black Sabbath growing up, Osbourne recalled times as a child when he would steal food from neighbors' vegetable gardens.

Despite the family's poverty, Osbourne said his parents worked very hard to ensure that their children had basic necessities like food and clothes.

Osbourne said, "There was never much money about, but they never let me or my brothers and sisters go without the essentials. And they gave us the best they had under the circumstances."[1]

As a child, Osbourne was restless and mischievous. He was given the nickname Ozzy at school, a play on words on his surname. He was the class clown at his grammar school, where he showed early signs of his wild side and love for entertaining.

Recalling his youth, Osbourne said, "When I was a child

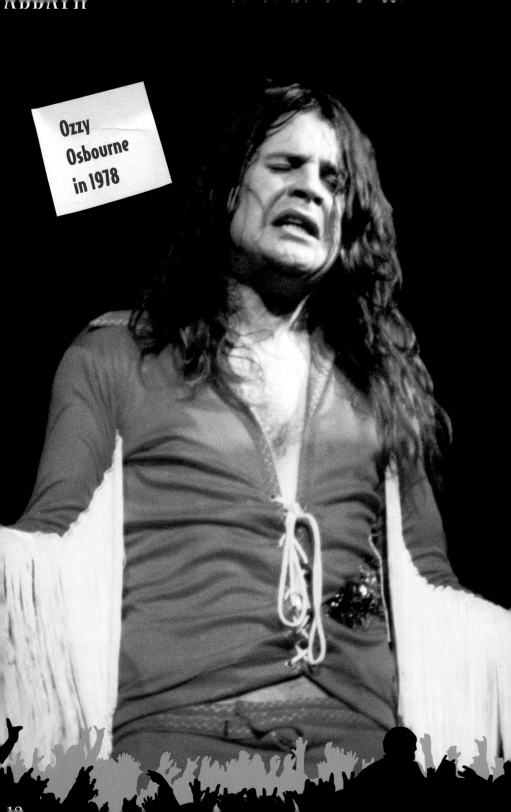

Ozzy
Osbourne
in 1978

at school, if people were miserable around me, I'd do some crazy things like jump through doorways, anything to make them amused, because I hated to see sad faces."[2]

The young Osbourne put his love of entertaining to good use in school musicals, participating in productions of Gilbert and Sullivan's *H.M.S. Pinafore, The Pirates of Penzance,* and *The Mikado.*[3]

But Osbourne did not show much of an interest in school. He was frequently in trouble with his teachers for cutting classes and failing grades. Osbourne was also insecure and bullied by older children.

Ironically, Osbourne remembers one young man in the next grade up named Tony Iommi who especially intimidated him. Iommi recalled, "I used to hate the sight of Ozzy. I couldn't stand him, and I used to beat him up whenever I saw him."[4]

At age fifteen, Osbourne left school to work as a tool-maker's apprentice, but quickly left the job. The same restlessness and inability to focus his attention that contributed to his lack of success at school followed Osbourne into the work world. He worked for a time assembling car horns at the same factory as his mother, and then left that job to become a plumber.

Osbourne said, "It was rather dreadful and everybody in my family worked in factories, really mindless jobs that were physically exhausting. My father, my mother, my sisters, they

all worked in factories in Birmingham and my dad thought I should become a tradesman to get a chance and better myself, get away from the factories."[5]

Osbourne's most infamous job was at a slaughterhouse, where he helped prepare animals for the butcher's shop. This job contributed to Osbourne's image later on in his career as a rock-and-roll wild man.

Osbourne soon tired of low-paying, physically demanding jobs and decided that it would be easier to steal than to work for a living. He began robbing clothing shops and then began breaking into people's homes. But Osbourne's life of crime did not last long: He and a friend were caught breaking into a home and arrested.

Osbourne's father could have paid a fine and kept his son out of jail, but he decided to teach his son a lesson instead. Mr. Osbourne refused to pay the fine and Osbourne spent six weeks in prison.

Placed among hardened criminals, Osbourne recalled being frightened and falling back on his penchant for making people laugh to avoid being roughed up. He said, "I got through a few hard times, and a lot of tough situations, by making people laugh and humoring them. I know six weeks doesn't sound like a lot, but it seemed like six years when I was in there."[6] It was during his time in jail that Osbourne tattooed the letters O-Z-Z-Y across his left knuckles.

Osbourne credited his father with teaching him a tough

but necessary lesson. By letting Osbourne go to jail instead of bailing him out, the elder Osbourne scared his son straight. Osbourne said, "Ultimately, perhaps my dad did the right thing by letting me go to prison. In some ways it was a good education for me. Because it showed me that the criminal life wasn't worth it."[7]

Once out of jail, Osbourne decided that he could pursue a career using his talent for entertaining people. He had always loved music, especially the Beatles. As a teenager, Osbourne said his room was "littered with Beatles stuff; I'd go 20 miles to get a poster of The Beatles."[8]

The Beatles' music, and the band's adoring fans, impressed Osbourne. The Beatles came from working-class families in the industrial city of Liverpool. The fact that the Beatles came from a similar background gave Osbourne hope that he, too, could make it big by playing in a band.

Speaking about the Beatles, Osbourne said, "I loved their music and I bought their records, but it was as much the fact that they were four guys like me who'd come from the back streets of Liverpool, opened all the doors, and proved it could be done."[9]

Because he could not play an instrument, Osbourne decided to become a singer. He placed an ad in a local music shop in 1968 that read: "Ozzy Zig Requires Gig. Owns own PA."[10]

The fact that Osbourne owned his own public address

system was a big draw for fellow musicians. It meant that a band would not have to pay to rent an amplification system to use at rehearsals and concerts. Soon Osbourne's ad would be answered, and the seeds of what would become Black Sabbath would take root.

Tony Iommi

Frank Anthony Iommi was born on February 19, 1948. His parents ran a general store. Iommi was an intimidating physical presence growing up. He was feared in the schoolyard and had thoughts of a professional fighting career. Iommi said, "My original ambition when I was small was to try martial arts, boxing, that sort of thing. I was always at the gym three or four times a week back then and I was a fanatic."[11]

Being physically fit was a plus in Birmingham. As Iommi explained, "Birmingham was very rough when we were growing up. There were gangs, and it was very hard to move away from that."[12]

Soon, however, Iommi started pumping his stereo more than he pumped iron. He said, "I started listening to music, and eventually all the physical stuff died off."[13]

Iommi started off on a most unheavy metal instrument: the accordion. He explained:

"Everyone else in my family played accordion, so I got one as well. In those days you used to just sit in your room and you didn't know what to do, so I learned to play accordion.

Tony Iommi
in 1977

From there I moved on to different instruments, and I eventually discovered the guitar."[14]

Influenced by such blues guitarists as John Mayall and a young Eric Clapton, Iommi picked up the instrument easily and was a standout player—as well as one of the only left-handed guitarists—in Aston. He joined his first band, The Pursuers, at age fifteen.[15] One year later, Iommi left school to pursue music while working at factory jobs to earn money.

The young guitarist's first big break came in 1965, when he was playing with a band called the Rockin' Chevrolets. The band had received an offer to play concerts in Germany, and Iommi was excited at the prospect of traveling and having people in another country hear his music. This opportunity would be a major turning point in Iommi's life, though not for the reasons he had envisioned at the time.

In order to go to Germany with the Rockin' Chevrolets, Iommi had to leave his job at the machine factory where he was working. On his last day at the job, Iommi came home on his lunch break and told his mother that he did not plan on returning for the afternoon shift. Iommi's mother, however, insisted that her son fulfill his responsibility to his employer. Iommi returned to work after lunch. By the end of the day, his life would change forever.

On that final afternoon, Iommi was working at a machine that pressed sheet metal. His job was to grab the metal pieces and move them down the assembly line. At one point he did

not pull his right hand out from under the machine quickly enough. The giant press dropped on Iommi's hand, chopping off the tops of his fingertips on his middle and ring fingers.

Iommi was in immense pain, but the physical pain would pale in comparison to the despair the guitarist felt when he was told that the injury had ended his dreams of becoming a professional musician.

Because Iommi is a left-handed guitarist, he uses his right fingertips to grip the guitar strings and play notes and chords. After the accident, it was too painful for Iommi to grasp the guitar strings. Several doctors told Iommi that he would never play again.[16]

Iommi was heartbroken and became depressed. His dream of becoming a successful guitarist appeared crushed in the freak accident. Iommi recalled, "All my hopes had gone down the drain. I really wanted to play and I couldn't. I got really depressed for a period."[17]

Iommi's spirits were lifted when his former boss at the sheet metal factory brought him a record by renowned jazz guitarist Django Reinhardt. At first Iommi could not understand why his friend would want him to hear another guitar player. It seemed to be a cruel reminder of what Iommi might have been able to accomplish before his accident.

But there was a specific reason why Iommi's friend wanted him to hear the record. Reinhardt had lost the ability to use two of the fingers on his left hand in a fire. Like Iommi, he did

not have full ability in the hand that grasps the guitar strings. Yet Reinhardt created his own style of playing with his remaining fingers and went on to have a successful career.

This inspired Iommi, who said that, "after hearing Django, I just wouldn't accept defeat. I was sure there had to be a way around my problem."[18] Iommi set to work finding a way to continue playing. Here, his inventive nature would come in handy.

Iommi created synthetic, plastic tips for his fingers. First, he melted a plastic medicine bottle into a small, round ball. He then used a hot soldering iron to shape the plastic to fit his fingers and filed it down with sandpaper to an appropriate size.

Though he could now play guitar again, Iommi found he still had limitations and would have to adjust his playing style. This change would help define Black Sabbath's unique sound.

Iommi found it easier to grip the guitar strings if he loosened them, so he tuned his guitar a half step lower than standard tuning. The lower tuning made his chords sound deeper and heavier than other rock-and-roll guitarists. Today, the technique is known as down-tuning and is a major characteristic of heavy metal music.

After returning to the music scene, Iommi joined a band called Mythology, which also included a drummer named Bill Ward, who recalled: "Tony came into that band and he was so

good. He was one of the best players in Birmingham and he was only 16."[19]

When Mythology broke up in 1968, Iommi and Ward stuck together and began to seek out players for a new band. Their pursuit intersected with a similar search by Osbourne and a bass player named Geezer Butler.

Geezer Butler

Terence Michael Joseph Butler was born on July 17, 1949. Butler was the youngest of three boys.

Butler's older brothers both served in the Army, where they picked up the term "geezer," which is a British slang word used to describe a good man, similar to the American phrase, "cool dude."

The youngest Butler explained that when his brothers came home on leave, "they'd be calling everybody a geezer. Then, of course, I picked it up and when I went to school I'd be calling everybody it."[20] Soon the name was applied to Butler, and Terry Butler would forevermore be known as Geezer.

Butler was raised in a strict, Irish-Catholic household and was fascinated with religion, at one point thinking he might become a priest. Butler read all kinds of books on religion, and "that developed into sort of wanting to know more about other religions, and other spirituality, more about the occult and everything else."[21]

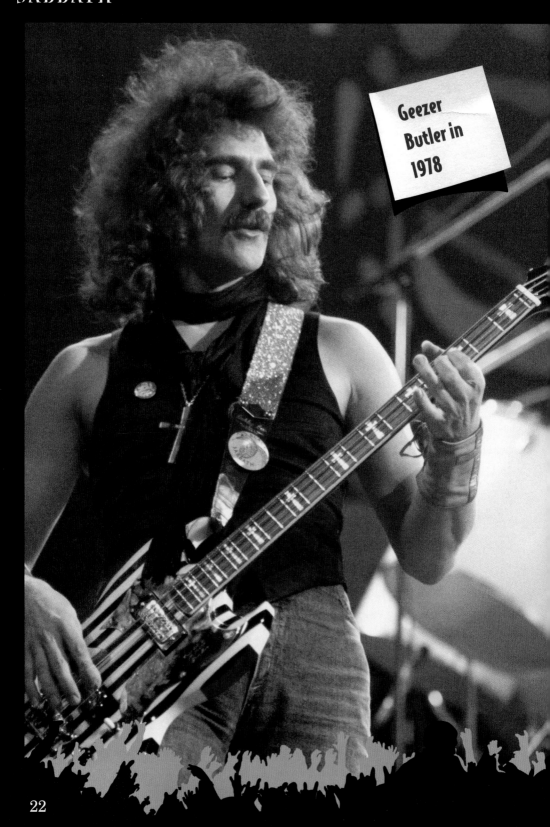

Geezer Butler in 1978

Butler's interest in spirituality would later find an outlet in the lyrics of many Black Sabbath songs, including "After Forever," "Black Sabbath," and "Lord of This World."

Like Osbourne, Butler loved the Beatles. Butler said, "It was four people from exactly the same background as where I was from, being able to rule the world. It gave everybody that was from the working classes in England some hope."[22]

Butler began his rock music career as a guitarist but switched to bass guitar after being mesmerized by Jack Bruce, the innovative and immensely talented bassist from the band Cream, which also featured guitar legend Eric Clapton. Bruce was one of the first bass players to pluck the instrument's strings with his fingers instead of using a pick.

Butler recalled the effect that watching Bruce had on his decision to become a bass player: "Bass players used to just stand there and use the pick, be in the background; you would never notice them, and then when I went to see Cream, it was so different to anybody else I had ever seen. I'd never seen anybody use the fingers before, and just his whole presence on stage . . . was amazing to me."[23]

In 1968, Butler was playing in a band called Rare Breed whose singer had just left the group. He saw the Ozzy Zig advertisement at the local record shop and contacted Osbourne about joining Rare Breed. However, Rare Breed broke up before anything more could happen. But Butler and Osbourne became friends and decided to form their own band. It was at

that time that Iommi and a drummer named Bill Ward also answered the Ozzy Zig ad.

Bill Ward

William Thomas Ward was born on May 5, 1948. He came from a musical family and began banging on a neighbor's drum-kit as early as age five. Ward said, "My mother played piano and my father sang, so the drummer who lived on the corner would bring his kit over on the weekend and we would have a party."[24]

As a child, Ward listened to the big band music of Count Basie, Benny Goodman, and Glenn Miller that his parents enjoyed. He was also influenced by his brother's Elvis Presley and Little Richard records.

While Osbourne and Butler's first musical love was the Beatles, Ward favored Presley. He said, "When I heard 'Jailhouse Rock,' something connected with me. I knew I wanted to sing and play in a rock-and-roll band."[25]

Though Ward has made his name primarily as a drummer, he has also been a singer. Ward sang lead vocals on the Black Sabbath songs "It's Alright" from the *Technical Ecstasy* album and "Swinging the Chain" on the *Never Say Die* album. He also sang on his two solo albums.

After leaving school at age fifteen, Ward, like Osbourne and Iommi, began working in a factory. He also delivered coal, all the while dreaming of making it big as a rock-and-roll star.

Bill
Ward in
the 1970s

The first step in making that dream become a reality came when Ward joined Iommi in the band Mythology. The group had built a small following but ultimately broke up, leaving Iommi and Ward to form their own band. That band would become Black Sabbath.

FROM BIRMINGHAM TO THE BIG TIME

T he members of Black Sabbath first came together in 1968, during the height of the hippie movement in the United States, where young people embraced music that spoke in favor of peace, love, and "flower power," and flocked to the Woodstock music festival.

But life in the late 1960s was a lot different across the Atlantic Ocean in Birmingham, England. Though the young men of Black Sabbath were anti-war and dressed the hippie part, with flowing locks and colorful outfits, their vision of the future was decidedly bleak.

In his book *Bang Your Head,* David Konow described the band's less-than-sunny out-look this way: "The members of Black

DURING THE 1960s, BIRMINGHAM, ENGLAND, WAS A BUSY, INDUSTRIAL CITY.

Sabbath may have looked like hippies with their long, wavy hair parted down the middle and their huge bell-bottoms swallowing up their feet, but there was nothing peaceful or flowery about their music."[1]

Black Sabbath's music and lyrics were influenced heavily by the band members' upbringing in postwar Birmingham, an industrial city that held little promise for the poor and working class beyond a monotonous life working in the factories.

Ozzy Osbourne recalled, "Everyone else was into flower power. It really made me angry and sick. It was all right for rich hippies living in California to sing about things like that, but what did we, living in Birmingham without two pennies to rub together, have to do with any of that?"[2]

For the members of Black Sabbath, music was a way to escape everyday boredom. If they were lucky, they might be the next Beatles, who rose from similar working-class roots in industrial Liverpool to become world famous. Geezer Butler stated, "When we started out we didn't ever think of making and selling albums anyway. It was just like a hobby to us, anything to avoid the nine to five jobs."[3]

In 1968, Tony Iommi and Bill Ward's band, Mythology, had broken up, and Butler's group, Rare Breed, was looking for a new singer. At the same time, Osbourne, calling himself Ozzy Zig, was looking to join a band and placed an advertisement in a local record shop.

Osbourne said the odd-sounding name was meant to get attention. He said, "I used to call myself Ozzy Zig because I thought it sounded cool and I thought everybody would start asking who Ozzy Zig was."[4]

Butler was the first to answer Osbourne's advertisement.

However, Rare Breed broke up before Osbourne had a chance to meet with the group.

At the same time, Iommi and Ward were looking to put a new band together following the demise of Mythology. They also saw the Ozzy Zig notice in the music shop. Iommi wondered if this could be the same Ozzy whom he had bullied at school. He hoped it was not, given his dislike for Osbourne's clownish ways at school. Iommi said, "I couldn't stand him. . . . [H]e was a real pain."[5]

Iommi did not recall Osbourne being a singer and thought the name was a coincidence. He found out differently when he and Ward visited the address listed on the poster and met "Ozzy Zig." Iommi said, "It was ironic how we ended up in the same band . . . but me and Bill were in a band and we were looking for a singer."[6]

Osbourne agreed to join forces with Iommi and Ward. Now the trio needed a bass player, and Osbourne recommended his friend Butler. The band, which also included a second guitar player and a saxophone player, was not immediately known as Black Sabbath.

At first the group called itself the Polka Tulk Blues Band, an eye-catching if unusual name. Osbourne came up with the name, though he cannot remember its origin.

By Iommi's account, the Polka Tulk Blues Band's first practices together were not memorable. Iommi recalled, "What a noise it was. It just sounded horrible. But we persevered."[7]

After a short time together the band fired its second guitar player and saxophonist while also shortening its name to Polka Tulk. Then came another name change, to the Earth Blues Band, which was subsequently shortened to Earth.

Most of the young bands in Birmingham—including Earth—played blues-based rock, influenced by such popular groups as the Beatles, the Who, and Cream. The 12-bar blues is the most basic form of rock music and relatively easy to play for beginners, so most young bands found themselves cutting their teeth on the blues. Butler explained: "We used to do a lot of Willie Dixon songs, Howlin' Wolf, Lightnin' Hopkins, and Muddy Waters. They were easy to play. When we first came

BEFORE BLACK SABBATH, OZZY OSBOURNE AND TONY IOMMI WERE IN A BAND CALLED EARTH.

together we formed in one day and had a gig a week later! We had never played together so we learned 18 12-bar blues numbers in a week."[8]

Earth nearly broke up when Iommi left the band in late 1968 to join the already established group Jethro Tull. Iommi had auditioned for Jethro Tull at the suggestion of a friend. Though Iommi wanted to continue playing with Earth, joining Jethro Tull, which had already released an album, was considered an opportunity that was too good to turn down.

Iommi's first order of business was to appear with Jethro Tull in the Rolling Stones concert movie, *The Rolling Stones Rock and Roll Circus*. Still, Iommi was conflicted. He said, "After a few days of rehearsals, I didn't feel comfortable, and told Ian Anderson [Jethro Tull's lead singer], but they asked me to stay to do the *Rock and Roll Circus,* and I did."[9]

Iommi returned to Earth after filming. Though Iommi was only in Jethro Tull for a short time, the experience of playing in a professional group proved valuable. Jethro Tull went about its work in a business-like way, practicing several days a week at set times, whereas Earth had a more laid-back schedule.

When Iommi returned to Birmingham and his old band, he brought Jethro Tull's work ethic with him. Iommi said: "I learned that you've got to work at it. You have to rehearse. When I came back I made sure that everybody was up early in the morning and rehearsing. . . . [Jethro Tull] had a schedule

and they knew that they were going to work from this time till that time. I tried that with our band, and we got into doing it. It worked. Instead of just strolling in at any hour, it made it more like we were saying, 'let's do it!'"[10]

Around this time, Earth's music began to take on its own identity. The group was tired of playing the same blues-based rock as all the other bands in Birmingham. They began to play a more aggressive, louder style of music.

Iommi began writing guitar riffs that, while still based in the blues, had a more sinister sound to them, a sense of foreboding and darkness. At the same time, Butler began writing lyrics that explored serious topics such as war, religion, and drug abuse.

A pivotal moment in the band's career came as the group gathered outside its recording studio. Across the street, a movie theater was playing a 1963 horror film starring Boris Karloff, the famous actor known for his role as Frankenstein's monster. The name of the movie was *Black Sabbath*. A poster advertising the film featured young people running in fear from a headless horseman holding a severed head.

At that moment, Osbourne said the band thought to itself out loud, "'[I]sn't it funny that people like to go and pay money to be scared, to see a horror film? Why don't we try and put that to some of this heavy stuff we're playing.'"[11]

Soon after this revelation, the band wrote a song called "Black Sabbath." It was an ominous number based on three

The band soon changed its name to Black Sabbath after seeing a movie poster. This film still is from the 1963 movie *Black*

eerie guitar notes and the lyrics told the story of a man who appeared to be possessed by a demon. Iommi said the song was a reference point for the band's new music. He said, "We knew it was good—and different."[12]

The band's new music had a lot of qualities in common with horror movies. Both explored dark subject matter and created a feeling of suspense that aimed to keep the viewer, or the listener, wondering what would come next.

When Earth began playing the song "Black Sabbath" at their shows, people were not sure what to think. Iommi said, "When we first tried out that song in the blues clubs, you could see the reaction on people's faces. They just stopped and stared in disbelief. 'What is that?' Then they'd come up and say, 'What was that song? Play it again!' We knew then we had something special."[13]

Around this time, the band decided to change its name once again. There was another band called Earth that had become popular at the time. The other Earth was a pop band, and it was not long before people began confusing the Earth who played an outrageous new form of music with the already established, softer group.

Butler described an incident in which his band turned up for a concert where the audience was expecting the other Earth to perform. He said, "There were all these older men and women, all dressed up nicely, suits and dresses. Then we started playing and the promoter came up and told us to shut up."[14]

While riding a ferry to Germany for a series of concerts in the summer of 1969, the men of Earth decided to change their band's name. They had already written a song that fit their music perfectly, and now it was to become their name: Black Sabbath.

In Germany, Osbourne wrote a letter to his mother that, looking back, was quite prophetic. He wrote, "We just changed the name of the band from Earth to Black Sabbath, maybe we'll make the big time now."[15]

Because the band had already been booked as Earth in Germany, it did not play its first official show as Black Sabbath until August 30, 1969, in Worcestershire, England.[16]

The band honed its chops in Germany during a residency at the Star Club in Hamburg. The Star Club was known as the training ground for the Beatles, who played there several times in 1962 before releasing their first album.

Black Sabbath took up residency at the Star Club for one week. They played up to seven forty-five-minute sets per night, which gave the band plenty of practice to tighten their performance. They also wrote new songs while in Hamburg which they immediately tried out on stage.

The band recalled their time in Hamburg as a tough but valuable learning experience. Osbourne said, "Everyone ended up doing outrageously long solos to fill up all the gaps in the set, they had us booked to play so many bloody sets a night! And we used to play really loud, as loud as we could get it, trying to drown out all conversation in the club."[17]

Upon returning to England, Black Sabbath's manager had finally managed to get the band a record deal after being rejected on his first fourteen attempts. Black Sabbath was given one day—October 16, 1969—to record the album at Regent Sound Studios in London. Their budget was £500, the equivalent of about $825.

Luckily for Black Sabbath, dozens of live performances over the past year had prepared them to record their songs quickly. The album would simply be called *Black Sabbath*, an introduction to the band and its music. The record was released on February 13, 1970.

The album's cover reflected the band's sinister sound. It featured a gloomy photo of an old mill in the countryside, with a mysterious woman in the foreground. The mood of the first song, "Black Sabbath," was set with the sounds of a thunder clap followed by a steady rain as a mournful church bell tolled. Then came the opening, menacing notes.

The song "Black Sabbath" starts slow, building up to a sense of impending doom as a man realizes he cannot escape the evil demon that is after his soul. Though the song "Black Sabbath" is all doom and gloom, the band had not completely abandoned its blues roots.

The second song on the album, "The Wizard," is an

up-tempo number featuring an Osbourne harmonica solo. Another standout track, "N.I.B.," features a solid groove rooted in the blues. Rumors began to spread at the time that "N.I.B." stood for Nativity in Black, the birth of the devil. But the band has consistently said that the title is a reference to Ward's beard, which at the time resembled a pen nib, the part of a fountain pen that comes into contact with the ink.

Because of its name and its eerie, new sound, Black Sabbath was immediately linked by some people to those who practiced black magic and the occult. This view was furthered by the inverted cross pictured on the inside of the band's first album. But the band denied being evil or satanic. Butler explained: "Obviously that stuff came along with the band name. . . . Some of the lyrics are concerned with the occult, of course, but it's not like we came out with this huge black magic image or anything."[18]

Furthermore, Butler said the upside-down cross was placed inside the album by the record company, without the band's knowledge.[19]

The band was asked by its record company to record the song "Evil Woman," originally recorded by an American blues-rock band called Crow, for its first single. "Evil Woman" was one of two cover songs on the album, the other being a song called "Warning," which was originally recorded by a British group called the Aynsley Dunbar Retaliation. Black Sabbath's

first album would be its only record to feature other people's songs.

Black Sabbath far exceeded the band's modest expectations, hitting number eight in the British album charts and number twenty-three in the United States. The band toured England and parts of western Europe, including Germany, Denmark, Switzerland, and Scotland. Osbourne said, "When we came back from Europe, and found out that the album was doing really well, it all came as a complete surprise to us. We couldn't believe it."[20]

Iommi was also pleasantly surprised with the success of *Black Sabbath*. He said the band was "absolutely thrilled when we heard *Black Sabbath* was a big seller in America. We would have been pleased if the album was just a hit album in Birmingham—when we saw it selling so well in the states, it was fantastic."[21]

In June 1970, Black Sabbath headed back to Regent Sound Studios to record its second album. The record that resulted, *Paranoid,* would be the band's breakthrough, and today is regarded as one of the all-time great heavy metal records. The album features three of the most well known songs in all of heavy metal: "Paranoid," "War Pigs," and "Iron Man."

Paranoid was released in September 1970 and catapulted Black Sabbath to stardom. The album hit number one in

England and was number twelve on the American charts, where the group would tour for the first time.

"Paranoid," arguably Black Sabbath's most popular song, ironically was a last-minute addition to the album. Butler explained: "We'd finished the album and had packed up all our gear and the management said they needed an extra three or four minutes to put on the album. We said we didn't have anything."[22]

Ward continued the story: "We get back into the studio and Tony immediately came up with the main riff you hear in 'Paranoid.' And as we got around our instruments, we started to jam. We hadn't been jamming for more than five minutes and we started to get an arrangement. . . . Top to bottom, the whole song took about 25 minutes."[23]

"War Pigs," a slow and churning number, was inspired by the Vietnam War, which was being fought at the time. The song's lyrics reflect the band's feeling that the working class and poor always seemed to fight in wars started by more well-to-do politicians. The song's introduction features the menacing call of an air-raid siren accompanying a lumbering assault of guitar, bass, and drums.

"Iron Man" was a science-fiction story about a man who travels through time and features another well-known heavy riff. Another song on the album, "Hand of Doom," was about heroin addiction. References to war and drugs would become common themes in future Black Sabbath songs.

Butler said at the time, "That's what my poems are about, things that are happening now. War and paranoia, death and hate. It gets people to thinking about what's going on."[24]

Though the lyrics in such songs as "War Pigs" contain horrific imagery, they have the same anti-war message as more peaceful protest songs. By showing the horrors of war, the band hoped people would realize that war should be avoided at all costs.

Butler explained, "We certainly had seen enough violence in our lives and we were totally against being dragged into the Vietnam War—or any war. So, like all sensible people, we were peace-loving."[25]

The band's concert tour for *Paranoid* included its first visit to the United States. The band's first show in the United States was on October 30, 1970, at Glassboro State College (now Rowan University) in Glassboro, New Jersey. Black Sabbath would tour the United States for five months in 1970 and 1971, performing in and around major cities such as New York, Detroit, Cleveland, Kansas City, Miami, Los Angeles, San Francisco, and Seattle.

Black Sabbath's next album, *Master of Reality,* hit stores in July 1971 and further expanded the band's popularity and notoriety. The album's catchy first track, "Sweet Leaf," was an outward acknowledgment of the band's experimentation with illegal drugs.

"Sweet Leaf" was an ode to marijuana, the band's favorite

illegal drug at the time. Ironically, although the song talks about marijuana as a positive influence, drug abuse would later help destroy the original lineup. Not surprisingly, including a song about drugs on the album fueled the band's critics.

Other songs on *Master of Reality* also contributed to Black Sabbath's receiving a bad image in the press, though the band's lyrics were not always as negative as some people thought.

Such song titles as "Children of the Grave," and controversial lyrics about the pope being hanged in the song "After Forever," spurred the image of Black Sabbath as immoral devil worshippers.

The band, however, found being labeled evil to be outrageous. Osbourne said the group was never involved in devil worship, though they were approached by people who were interested in the occult. He said, "I remember when we started getting invites to black masses. We all looked at each other and said, 'Is this for real or what?'"[26]

A closer look at Black Sabbath's song lyrics reveals a more hopeful side to the band. "Children of the Grave," for example, despite sounding like the name of a horror movie, talks about the need for the next generation to bring peace and love to the world and to avoid nuclear war. While "After Forever" does mention the pope in a negative light, it also talks about God's love as a positive influence.

Despite, and in some cases because of, the controversy that surrounded the band, Black Sabbath's music continued to captivate fans. Iommi's guitar riffs were heavy, but they were also catchy and hummable. Combined with Butler's aggressive bass playing, Ward's powerful drumming, and Osbourne's nasally, instantly recognizable vocals, Black Sabbath was both powerful and unique.

Iommi said the band's songs "sounded different from anything anyone else was doing at that time."[27] He also said, "It had more of a dramatic, more powerful sound than other rock bands."[28]

By the time Black Sabbath finished touring for *Master of Reality,* they were one of the most popular rock bands of the day, headlining large halls and arenas in Europe and the United States. They were also partaking heavily in drugs and alcohol while on tour, with Osbourne and Ward the worst offenders. The band's decision to record its next album in the United States for the first time would continue this trend for the worse.

When it came time to write and record its fourth album in 1972, Black Sabbath chose sunny California over rainy London. The band rented a mansion in Beverly Hills and recorded the album in a Los Angeles studio, enjoying its newfound status as legitimate rock stars. Iommi said, "It was a lovely house, had a ballroom and everything, fantastic. There was a bar downstairs and we set up the equipment in there and just wrote the album."[29]

The writing and recording process was a significant change from the past. When Black Sabbath rehearsed and recorded in England, the band members worked in the studio during the day and returned home to their families at night. In California, the band was far away from family responsibilities and spent most of its time free time throwing parties at its mansion, where they continued to heavily abuse drugs and alcohol.

Ward especially was guilty of drug abuse. He said, "My cocaine addiction was pretty darn heavy." In fact, the whole band was abusing cocaine.[30]

Whereas Black Sabbath's previous album included "Sweet Leaf," a song about marijuana, its new album, titled *Volume IV,* included a song about cocaine called "Snowblind." It was a troubling development, given that cocaine is considered a more addictive and dangerous drug than marijuana.

Despite the distractions and increasing excess that came with recording in California, Black Sabbath managed to produce another exceptional album. *Volume IV* was released in September 1972 and included some of the band's heaviest and catchiest songs yet in "Snowblind" and "Wheels of Confusion" and, in a departure for the band, a gorgeous ballad called "Changes."

Speaking about the album in general and "Changes"

specifically, Osbourne said: "Our new album still has the Black Sabbath sound, but it's more melodic. I'm singing different melodic things and it's all building up. ["Changes"] is a nice piece of music."[31]

Volume IV hit number eight on the British charts and number thirteen in the United States. With the band's popularity growing across the world, Black Sabbath played its first

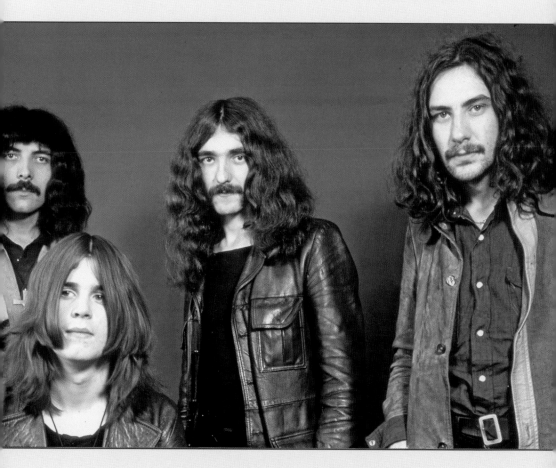

BLACK SABBATH IN 1973

shows in Australia and New Zealand while on tour for *Volume
IV* in early 1973.

Though Iommi was the least involved in drugs among
the band members, he had the toughest time getting ready to
record the band's next album. As Iommi sat down with his
guitar and prepared to write songs, he discovered that, for the
first time in his life, he had writer's block.

Iommi recalled, "I couldn't think of anything. . . . We had
a couple of songs, but not an album."[32]

Butler explained further, saying, "We had been in America
trying to write *Sabbath Bloody Sabbath,* but nothing was
working. We felt like we were on the verge of breaking up, so
we came back to England."[33]

Once back home, the band rented Clearwell Castle, in
southwest England near Wales, with plans to live there while
writing the next album. There would be no wild parties this
time around. The band would be left alone in peace to work on
their new material in the eighteenth-century castle.

Soon after Black Sabbath arrived at Clearwell Castle,
strange occurrences began happening that befitted the band's
evil image and creepy sound. Butler recalled one scary
moment: "We were in the dungeon playing away and all of a
sudden we saw this person walk past the door that had a big
black cloak on."[34]

Iommi and one of the band's assistants went running
after the figure, which entered another room. Butler continued,

"There was nobody in there; he totally disappeared. We asked the owner of the castle about it and he told us, 'Oh, that's just the ghost.' I went home every night after that."[35]

Was the castle haunted? Were the band members imagining things? Or were they playing practical jokes on one another? The band members would later admit to trying to scare each other, but through the years they have insisted that some strange, unexplained things happened at the castle.

Whatever the explanation, Black Sabbath, the scariest band in the world, was too scared to stay overnight in Clearwell Castle. They still wrote and rehearsed there, but drove home every night at the end of the day. Today, the castle does not appear to scare people. It is a popular site for weddings.

Despite, or perhaps because of, the weird atmosphere in Clearwell Castle, Black Sabbath crafted its strongest, most menacing album to date. Iommi broke through his writer's block like a wrecking ball crashing through a brick wall with the main riff to the song "Sabbath Bloody Sabbath." It is one of the most well-known and heaviest riffs in Black Sabbath history.

Butler said the riff was a turning point: "Tony came up with the riff for 'Sabbath Bloody Sabbath' and everybody sparked into life. I'll always remember that album and look back on it with a good feeling."[36]

The album's title, as well as its cover art, were attention grabbers. The album cover depicted a number of demons

cavorting over a man on his deathbed. The band may have sung about peace and love, but their image remained the opposite.

Again, as was the case with the band's lyrics, first looks were deceiving. The album cover was actually a warning against the perils of avarice. Osbourne said, "There are all these distorted figures bending over him and gloating as he lies there. These figures are actually him at different stages of his life. He's a man of greed, a man who's wanted everything all his life and done all this evil stuff."[37]

Sabbath Bloody Sabbath was released in December 1973. The title track was a blistering manifesto aimed at critical journalists and allegedly crooked managers that Black Sabbath felt had cheated them out of money. The title is a take on Bloody Sunday, an incident in Northern Ireland in which protesters were shot by British soldiers.[38]

The songs "Spiral Architect" and "A National Acrobat," with their complex arrangements, showcased the band's growing musical skill level. In a review of the album in *Rolling Stone* magazine, Gordon Fletcher wrote that *Sabbath Bloody Sabbath* "possesses a degree of internal intricacy that belies popular conceptions of heavy-metal. The use of tempo changes and electronic keyboards to cast liquid emotions makes *Sabbath Bloody Sabbath* an extraordinarily gripping affair."[39]

Sabbath Bloody Sabbath reached number four on the British charts and number eleven in the United States.

The band embarked on another successful headlining tour in 1974, including an appearance at the California Jam festival before two hundred thousand people.

Little did Black Sabbath know that the period around *Sabbath Bloody Sabbath* would be the original lineup's peak. The next few years would be spent hurtling toward a significant lineup change that would forever alter Black Sabbath's history.

In 1975, Black Sabbath had quite a few hits. They performed
many concerts throughout the world.

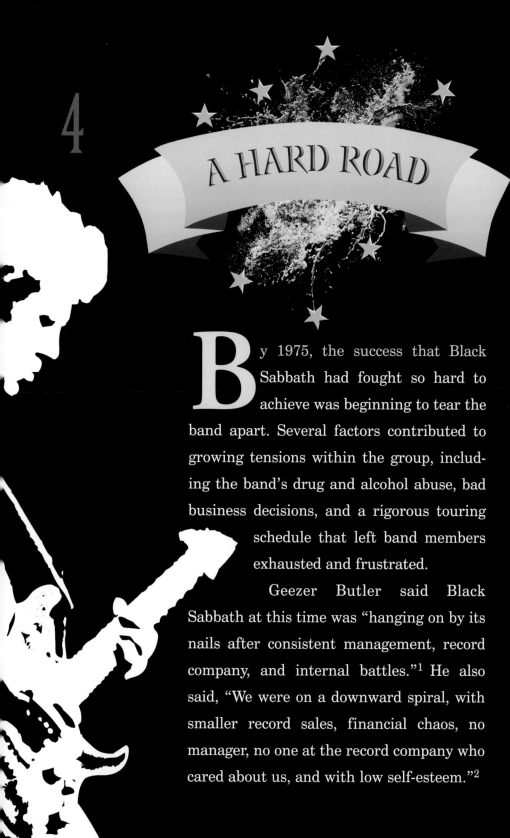

A HARD ROAD

4

By 1975, the success that Black Sabbath had fought so hard to achieve was beginning to tear the band apart. Several factors contributed to growing tensions within the group, including the band's drug and alcohol abuse, bad business decisions, and a rigorous touring schedule that left band members exhausted and frustrated.

Geezer Butler said Black Sabbath at this time was "hanging on by its nails after consistent management, record company, and internal battles."[1] He also said, "We were on a downward spiral, with smaller record sales, financial chaos, no manager, no one at the record company who cared about us, and with low self-esteem."[2]

Referring specifically to drug use, Butler said, "The more dependent we were on it the more the music suffered and the more we disagreed with each other, and in the end we didn't even speak to each other."[3]

Black Sabbath was easily taken advantage of financially. The band did not have any business experience and their drug abuse left them both vulnerable to signing bad contracts and not having the presence of mind to watch their bank accounts.

Butler said, "We'd sold millions of albums, sold out thousands of concerts, but we were not seeing the money."[4]

Ozzy Osbourne said the band never prepared for the business side of rock and roll. He said, "I entered rock-and-roll purely because of the fun angle and then all of the sudden there was a business side of it. We had to get involved in business somewhere. We didn't have a clue."[5]

Osbourne also said, "No one thought about royalties, publishing, merchandise and residuals because we were all too busy touring."[6]

Osbourne also began to see the band's seemingly endless touring in the United States much the same way he viewed the factory jobs he had hated as a youth. In a 1974 interview, Osbourne said, "I regard the States as my factory. . . . I go to America to clock on for work and after clocking off I go home to England to rest. But it doesn't get any easier the more you do it, in fact it seems to get harder!"[7]

The strain and exhaustion began creeping into the band's music on its sixth album, *Sabotage*. Released in July 1975, the album included several songs based on the band's negative experiences with the music industry.

The album's title was an allusion to the difficulty the band had making the record. They felt that legal and business troubles had conspired to sabotage Black Sabbath's ability to focus on recording.

The song "Megalomania" refers to the egos the band encountered in the music business. "The Writ"—the English term for a court action—was about Black Sabbath's legal troubles with its former managers, whom the band felt had cheated them out of earnings. The band and its former managers were suing each other, and Iommi recalled receiving subpoenas in the studio during this time.[8]

The band's overall state was best summed up by the song "Am I Going Insane (Radio)." The phrase "radio" was short for "radio-rental," which Ward said was slang for people who were mentally ill.[9]

Though Black Sabbath was dealing with inner turmoil, the band's troubles did not affect their music or their popularity. *Sabotage* did well in the charts, hitting number seven in England and number twenty-eight in the United States, and the band's concert tour for the album included a sold-out show at the world-famous Madison Square Garden in New York City.

But a change in the band's dynamic was coming. The nonstop cycle of making albums and touring over the past six years had left the band members physically and emotionally exhausted. They had been spending more time in recording studios and on the road than with their families.

The pressure was starting to become too much to handle, especially for Osbourne. Jezz Woodruffe, a keyboard player who worked with the band in the studio in the mid-1970s, said of Osbourne during that time period: "We had to drag him into the studio. We had to push him onto the stage when we were touring. He just wanted to go home."[10]

The band's decline began to show musically on the follow-up to *Sabotage,* 1976's *Technical Ecstasy.* The album, recorded in Miami, lacked the firepower, passion, and cohesion of the band's previous work.

Only one song, "Dirty Women," could be considered among the band's greatest hits. "Dirty Women" is about the prostitutes that the band would see on street corners while driving to the studio.

Another drug reference surfaced in the song "Rock 'N' Roll Doctor," about a doctor who provided the band with narcotics that were illegal to possess without a prescription. The ballad "It's Alright," which featured Bill Ward on lead vocals, failed to reach the heights of the band's previous slow song, "Changes."

Overall, *Technical Ecstasy* was missing the sinister guitar

parts and provocative vocals that fans had come to expect from Black Sabbath. Even the album cover, a modern-art piece depicting two robots, did not seem to make any sense.

Technical Ecstasy was the first Black Sabbath album that did not break the top ten in England, only reaching number thirteen. There was also a drastic decline in the United States, where *Technical Ecstasy* peaked on the charts at number fifty-one. Previously, Sabbath had done no worse than number twenty-eight.

In November 1977, Black Sabbath was about to begin work on its next album. But Osbourne, who was fed up with the endless touring and the negative effects it was having on his relationship with his first wife, Thelma, dropped a bombshell: He was quitting the band.

Osbourne said, "Everything had been going wrong with Sabbath, with my personal life, and with everything I touched I ended up having trouble. I was in a terrible state; I couldn't eat, I couldn't sleep."[11]

The rest of the band, weary of Osbourne's increasingly unpredictable behavior due to his drug and alcohol abuse, carried on without him. They recruited singer Dave Walker from the English blues-rock band Savoy Brown to become Black Sabbath's new singer.

Over the next two months, the band began the writing process with Walker for the next Black Sabbath album. They taped a performance with Walker on a British music television

show, but the program never aired. This would be Walker's only performance with Black Sabbath.

By January 1978, Osbourne decided he wanted to return to Black Sabbath. The band, which was not gelling musically with Walker, welcomed him back. Osbourne said, "I talked myself into going back. I didn't know what else I was going to do. But I knew in my heart of hearts that eventually I would leave again."[12]

The band welcomed Osbourne back, but Black Sabbath's problems did not disappear. Instead, they got worse. When he came back, Osbourne refused to perform any of the songs that the band had written with Walker.

This presented a major problem because the group had booked studio time in Toronto to record its new album. Osbourne's refusal to sing the new songs meant that Black Sabbath would have to start writing new songs at the same time it was scheduled to be in the recording studio.

Black Sabbath literally worked night and day in Toronto on its eighth album. Forced to write new songs at the last minute, the band would rehearse the new material during the day and return at night to record the songs.

The band had recorded in Toronto at Tony Iommi's insistence. He wanted the band to record there partly because the famous English rock group the Rolling Stones had made an album in the same studio. Iommi thought that recording in the same place as the Rolling Stones would inspire the band.

Osbourne, however, thought the idea was ridiculous. At this point in time Iommi was becoming more involved with the production of the band's albums. As a perfectionist, Iommi took his time recording, which frustrated Osbourne: "The last two Sabbath albums Tony would sit in the studio for days and days just tuning up! And all I wanted to do was get back to good basic hard rock. Our first few albums were started and finished and ready for release within a matter of weeks, but this thing was starting to take months."[13]

The rushed song-writing process, drawn-out recording, and Osbourne's general unhappiness combined to make for another disappointing effort. *Never Say Die!* was released in September 1978 and marked the band's tenth anniversary.

The album boasted an energetic and catchy title track, but the rest of the record was an uneven effort that saw Black Sabbath moving farther away from its heavy metal roots. *Never Say Die!* included more synthesizer parts than on past albums. The song "Swinging the Chain" featured a horn section while the instrumental track "Breakout" had a jazz feel to it.

Butler said *Never Say Die!* "wasn't very good, anyway. It was sort of thrown together at the last minute, and that's why it's so bad. I just don't like that album."[14]

In England, *Never Say Die!* fared better than *Technical Ecstasy,* reaching number twelve on the charts. In the United

States, it only placed as high as number sixty-nine, Black Sabbath's worst chart showing in the band's history.

Though the band continued to play to sold-out audiences on its ten-year anniversary tour in support of *Never Say Die!*, the band itself admitted that it was showing signs of fatigue and disinterest on stage. Osbourne said, "By the time the album was finally finished and we went out for that last tour there was no spark left whatsoever."[15]

Making things worse, the energetic young band called Van Halen that opened the shows received, at times, more favorable reviews than Black Sabbath. Van Halen, who has gone on to sell millions of albums, was just starting out and showed the hunger that Black Sabbath had lost.

Osbourne said the tour was a "disaster" because "Van Halen was opening for us and . . . they were great and we were just falling apart on stage every night."[16]

The final show of the tour, on December 11, 1978, in Albuquerque, New Mexico, would be the last time the original lineup played together for seven years.

In 1979, Osbourne once again left Black Sabbath—only this time he did not walk away on his own. Iommi, Butler, and Ward had had enough of the singer's drug and alcohol problems and the unpredictable behavior, uneven performances, and occasional cancelled concert that resulted. As the group prepared to record its next album, the decision was made to fire Osbourne.

The young band Van Halen had once opened for Black Sabbath. Van Halen in 1978 was, from left to right: Eddie Van Halen, David Lee Roth, Alex Van Halen, and Michael Anthony.

Butler said of Osbourne, "He was in a really bad state at the time and he just couldn't get himself together. He wasn't turning up at the band rehearsals or the recording sessions. On the last tour he kept disappearing and was always drunk. I think it turned out for the best for all of us."[17]

Iommi said that Osbourne was "totally out of control"[18] and that the band had reached a crossroads: "It had to come to either what are we going to do, break up or replace Ozzy."[19]

Ward, who was Osbourne's best friend in the band, delivered the bad news. Ward said, "I felt incredibly sad. I knew that it would have to be me that would have to tell Oz the news. And it was. But I tried to tell him as gently as I could. I broke my heart that day."[20]

Osbourne admitted later that his heart was no longer in the band: "None of us were really into it anymore. . . . Something had to give and I suppose it was me. I really wasn't putting any effort into it and neither was anyone else."[21] He characterized the breakup as a "sad, and a really depressing end."[22]

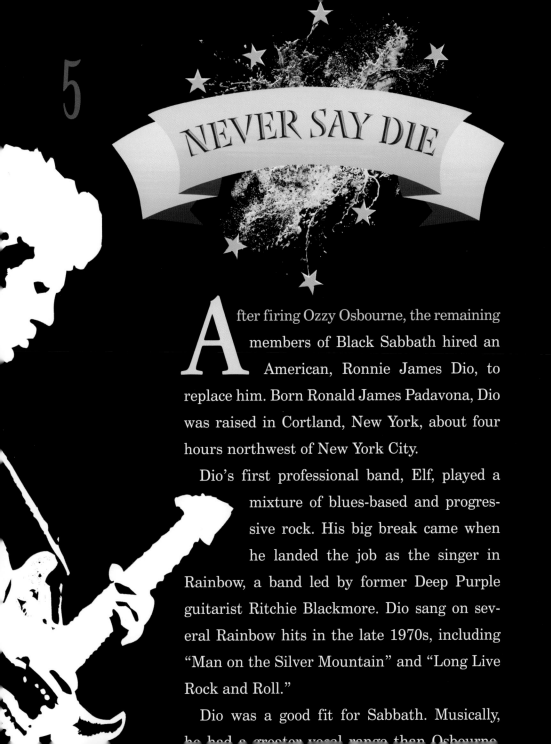

NEVER SAY DIE

After firing Ozzy Osbourne, the remaining members of Black Sabbath hired an American, Ronnie James Dio, to replace him. Born Ronald James Padavona, Dio was raised in Cortland, New York, about four hours northwest of New York City.

Dio's first professional band, Elf, played a mixture of blues-based and progressive rock. His big break came when he landed the job as the singer in Rainbow, a band led by former Deep Purple guitarist Ritchie Blackmore. Dio sang on several Rainbow hits in the late 1970s, including "Man on the Silver Mountain" and "Long Live Rock and Roll."

Dio was a good fit for Sabbath. Musically, he had a greater vocal range than Osbourne

Ronnie James Dio (bottom right) was soon hired to replace Osbourne which gave the band more variety in its music. Geezer Butler said, "Ronnie brought a lot to the band at a time when we needed it. He gave the band a whole lease on life. He gave everybody inspiration!"[1]

Unlike Osbourne, Dio took good care of himself physically. He did not abuse drugs or alcohol, he could be relied upon to show up on time for rehearsals and interviews, and to be at his best for concerts and studio recordings. Tony Iommi said, "Ronnie really came in as a professional. We were able to sit down and write the album without any problems."[2]

Dio held no illusions about being able to make fans forget about Osbourne, but he also displayed confidence in his abilities to help Black Sabbath. He said: "I was not and never will be Ozzy Osbourne. He was the vocalist and songwriter in that era who helped create that band . . . in its classic form. But at that time Sabbath was a band that was floundering, and with my inclusion in it we pulled ourselves up by our bootstraps, cared a lot about each other, and knew that we could do it again."[3]

As they set about recording their first album with Dio in 1980, Black Sabbath had something to prove: That they could succeed without Osbourne.

Butler recalled, "We were written off by everyone." He said that when Osbourne was fired critics told him, "Black Sabbath is Ozzy, and you can't carry on without Ozzy."[4]

Osbourne, meanwhile, was angry about being fired and

that the band decided to keep the Black Sabbath name. He said at the time, "I just feel sorry for them if that is the situation they want to get into."[5]

Titled *Heaven and Hell,* Black Sabbath's debut with Dio was released in May 1980 and followed by an extensive tour. The album was generally well received by fans and the press. On the charts, *Heaven and Hell* reached number nine in England and number twenty-eight in the United States.

Sabbath followed up *Heaven and Hell* with another strong effort, 1981's *Mob Rules,* which reached number twelve in England and number twenty-nine in the United States.

Mob Rules also featured a new band member. Vinny Appice had replaced Bill Ward, who left the band during the *Heaven and Hell* tour. Ward's alcohol and drug abuse, coupled with his unhappiness in playing without his close friend Osbourne, proved too much for him to take.

Ward said, "It just didn't feel right and it never has felt right and I've never been able to play comfortably in any other Black Sabbath other than with Ozzy, Tony, and Geezer."[6]

As the eighties unfolded and led into the nineties, Black Sabbath's fortunes waned with each passing year as more than a dozen lineup changes between 1983 and 1991 weakened the band's identity. In several versions of Black Sabbath during this time, Iommi was the only original member.

Sabbath's downfall began when Dio and Appice left the

band in 1982. Dio was replaced by former Deep Purple singer Ian Gillan, and Ward returned to play drums.

Throughout the next fifteen years, Sabbath became a revolving door for musicians. These included Deep Purple singer Glenn Hughes; drummers Bev Bevan of Blue Oyster Cult and Terry Chimes of the Clash; Whitesnake bass player Neil Murray; and the late drummer Cozy Powell of Rainbow, Whitesnake, and the Jeff Beck Group.

With Black Sabbath changing personnel so often, it was hard for fans to keep track of who was in the band and to become attached to the group. The new versions of Black

BY THE MID-1980s, BLACK SABBATH HAD GONE THROUGH MANY BAND MEMBERS. FROM LEFT TO RIGHT: GEOFF NICHOLLS, TONY IOMMI, DAVE SPITZ, ERIC SINGER, AND GLENN HUGHES.

Sabbath could no longer sell out large concert halls or millions of records.

As a further insult, the band's unsuccessful attempt to use the Stonehenge monument as a stage prop during its 1983 *Born Again* tour was spoofed in the 1984 mock documentary, *This Is Spiñal Tap*. In the film, the fictional band Spiñal Tap orders an eighteen-foot-high model of a Stonehenge rock to be lowered onto the stage during its set. But the model that comes down during the concert is only eighteen inches high, much to the band's dismay and embarrassment.

In real life, the opposite had happened. Black Sabbath had ordered a fifteen-foot-tall model of the famous stone. But the prop company misread the order as fifteen meters (forty-five feet). The massive prop that resulted was too large to be used.

Butler said, "It was 45 feet high and it wouldn't fit on any stage anywhere so we just had to leave it in the storage area. It cost a fortune to make but there was not a building on earth that you could fit it into."[7]

Though some fans criticized Iommi for keeping the name Black Sabbath without any original members, the guitarist defended his actions. He explained, "I didn't want to see Black Sabbath just fall by the wayside. I've been in Black Sabbath since the beginning, so I didn't see any reason to say, 'that's it, that's the end.' I just wanted to carry on."[8]

Ozzy Osbourne in the 1980s

6

BLIZZARD OF OZZ

Although Black Sabbath quickly regrouped with Ronnie James Dio after firing Ozzy Osbourne, the band's former singer was not able to move on with his life as easily. Following his dismissal from Black Sabbath, Osbourne spiraled into a deep depression. He spent the first few months after being fired holed up in a Los Angeles hotel room where he drank heavily every day. Osbourne said, "When I left Sabbath I was in total turmoil in the mind."[1]

It was during this low point in Osbourne's life when his future wife entered the picture. Sharon Arden was the daughter of Osbourne's manager, Don Arden, and her job was to check in on Osbourne after his firing.

It was Sharon who prodded Osbourne to stop feeling sorry for himself and form his own band.

Osbourne said, "I was in a state of shock . . . until my wife came into my life and said, 'you clean your act up.' I thought I might as well have the biggest party in my life because I'm back to the unemployment line."[2] Osbourne and Sharon Arden married on July 4, 1982.

Sharon Osbourne is widely credited with reviving her husband's career. Rudy Sarzo, who joined Osbourne's solo band in 1981, said, "I can honestly tell you that if it wasn't for her, the band never would have happened."[3]

With Sharon's help, Osbourne got back on his feet and discovered a guitarist named Randy Rhoads in California. Two veteran English musicians, bassist Bob Daisley and drummer Lee Kerslake, were recruited to round out Osbourne's new solo band.

Osbourne was motivated to show the world that he was still a musical force and could succeed without Sabbath. His debut solo album, *Blizzard of Ozz,* proved him right. The album, which is now considered a heavy metal classic, arrived in September 1980 to positive reviews. *Blizzard of Ozz* hit number seven on the charts in England and twenty-one in the United States. *Blizzard of Ozz* charted higher in England and the United States than Black Sabbath's first post-Osbourne album, *Heaven and Hell*.

Osbourne's 1981 album, *Diary of a Madman,* also fared

well with critics and fans, reaching number sixteen on the charts in England and number fourteen in the United States. Osbourne was riding high, but his career, and personal life, would soon be derailed by tragedy.

On March 19, 1982, Randy Rhoads was killed in a plane crash while the band was on tour. Rhoads and the band's wardrobe manager, Rachael Youngblood, had gone for a ride on a small plane piloted by the band's bus driver during an early morning stop in Florida while the rest of the group slept in the tour bus. The pilot lost control of the plane, which crashed into the garage of a nearby home, killing all three on board.

Though only twenty-five years old when he died, Rhoads was already seen as an influential guitarist for his mixing elements of classical music in heavy metal. Many hard rock and heavy metal guitarists cite Rhoads today as an influence. Osbourne was devastated but vowed to carry on.

Osbourne rebounded from his loss and became a superstar in the years and decades that followed. He toured the world, performed in front of millions of adoring fans, and sold more than 20 million albums in the United States alone.

Osbourne also became known for his wild antics, which usually occurred when he drank too much. In one well-publicized incident, Osbourne bit the head off of a live bat that had been thrown onstage during a 1982 concert in Iowa.

Osbourne, who received a round of painful rabies shots afterward, explained that he thought the bat was a plastic toy.

In another notorious event, Osbourne was arrested for being publicly intoxicated and urinating on the Alamo, a historical landmark, in San Antonio, Texas. Osbourne was subsequently banned from playing in San Antonio for life, though the restriction was lifted after twenty years.

Osbourne also developed a knack for finding talented young guitarists. After Rhoads died, Osbourne enlisted Jake E. Lee, a flashy guitarist from California. Lee played on Osbourne's 1986 hit single, "Shot in the Dark." In the late 1980s, Osbourne discovered New Jersey native Zakk Wylde, who has been his guitarist for the past twenty years and fronts his own band, Black Label Society. Geezer Butler would reunite with Osbourne to play bass in his solo band for a short period in the late 1980s.

All but one of Osbourne's solo albums since 1986 have hit the top five on the American charts. Hit songs such as "Crazy Train," "Bark at the Moon," and "Mama, I'm Coming Home," are still heard regularly on hard rock radio stations today.

Osbourne became so popular that in 1996 he started a traveling heavy metal festival, dubbed the Ozzfest. The annual Ozzfest would become a top-selling tour and introduce Osbourne to a new generation of fans.

Ozzfest also served as a launching point for several popular bands. Slipknot, System of a Down, and Incubus all

In 2002, *The Osbournes* aired on MTV. From left to right: Ozzy, Sharon Osbourne (standing), Jack Osbourne (sitting on floor), and Kelly Osbourne.

received their first widespread exposure through the Ozzfest. Speaking about his, and Black Sabbath's influence on younger bands, Osbourne said, "So many kids in these new bands . . . at the Ozzfest, when I'm walking down the street or whatever, they say, 'I owe my life to you and Sabbath.'"[4]

Osbourne became an even bigger star in 2002 with the premiere of the MTV reality show, *The Osbournes*. The show followed the lives of Osbourne, his wife, and their teenage children in their Beverly Hills mansion and on the road. Osbourne was seen as a goofy, likable dad befuddled by basic household tasks such as operating his home theater system's remote control.

Tony Iommi joked about fans getting a glimpse of Osbourne's home life: "It's funny. Finally people are seeing what we have for 35 years. Now they know what we've been moaning about."[5]

The Osbournes, which ran until 2005, was a huge success. It gained the highest ratings for any show in MTV's history and won the 2002 Emmy Award for Outstanding Reality Program.

In 2003, Osbourne and his then nineteen-year-old daughter Kelly scored a number-one hit on the English pop charts with their duet of the Black Sabbath ballad, "Changes." The song hit the top of the charts less than a week after Osbourne was seriously injured in an all-terrain vehicle on his estate in England. He sustained numerous injuries, including several broken ribs, but made a full recovery.

Osbourne released his latest solo album, *Black Rain,* in May 2007. The record reached number three on the American charts and number eight in England.

REUNITED

Despite stating that they did not wish to perform together any longer after their initial break-up, the original members of Black Sabbath reunited on July 13, 1985, for a one-time appearance at the historic Live Aid charity concert in Philadelphia.

Live Aid was a massive, all-star benefit to raise money to feed starving children in the African country of Ethiopia. Two concerts were performed on the same day, one in Philadelphia and one in London. Many top acts of the time performed, including Sting, the Who, Queen, Elton John, Bryan Adams, Madonna, and Led Zeppelin.

Black Sabbath was one of the first bands

to play in Philadelphia, performing at the very un-rock-and-roll time of 10:00 in the morning. The group's fifteen-minute set consisted of "Children of the Grave," "Iron Man," and "Paranoid."

Ozzy Osbourne made clear at the time that he had no desire to give up his solo career for a full-fledged Black Sabbath reunion. He said at the time, "I'm telling you now, it ain't gonna happen! No way."[1]

The band members went their separate ways after Live Aid, but, contrary to Osbourne's statements at the time, it would not be the last time they shared a stage.

The next step toward a full-fledged reunion of the original Black Sabbath came when Tony Iommi, Geezer Butler, and Bill Ward joined Osbourne onstage in Costa Mesa, California, in 1992 for a special encore at what was billed as Osbourne's final solo show before his retirement—a retirement that has yet to happen. The band played "Black Sabbath," "Fairies Wear Boots," "Iron Man," and "Paranoid," to a wild reception.

Earlier that year, the Dio-Iommi-Butler-Appice lineup of Black Sabbath had reunited and released an album, *Dehumanizer*. Originally, Black Sabbath, with Ronnie Dio singing, was supposed to open the Costa Mesa show. But Dio refused, and Judas Priest singer Rob Halford filled in. Dio thought that opening for Osbourne would be embarrassing and make the new Black Sabbath seem less important.

Dio said, "Here we were trying to get [Black Sabbath] back on the road together, trying to reform this band and make it special again, and now, suddenly, we were going to be the opening act for the ex-lead singer."[2]

Dio was so upset that Sabbath played with Osbourne again that he left the band. He sensed that the original lineup would eventually get back together, and he was right.

To the delight of Black Sabbath fans worldwide, Osbourne announced that Butler and Iommi would join him to play encores during his Ozzfest shows in the summer of 1997. Mike Bordin, then the drummer from Osbourne's solo band, filled in for Ward, who was not invited for health reasons.

Although this was not the complete original lineup, fans were ecstatic. Those who were too young to see the original Black Sabbath now had an opportunity to see what they never thought would be possible: Osbourne, Iommi, and Butler onstage together. Longtime fans who had given up hope that they would ever see the original band play together again were also thrilled.

The final piece of the puzzle was completed in December 1997 when Ward, who was back in good health, joined the rest of the band for two shows in Black Sabbath's hometown of Birmingham, England. The shows were recorded for a live album titled *Reunion* and a DVD called *The Last Supper*.

There was not one specific reason for the reunion. The band simply felt the time was right. According to Osbourne:

Black Sabbath in 1998. Ozzy Osbourne is sitting; in the back from left to right are: Bill Ward, Tony Iommi, and Geezer Butler.

"We'd suddenly found that we'd missed each other. It wasn't like a band reunion, it was like a family reunion. Emotionally over the years we've had our ups and downs, but we'd still been very close."[3]

Butler was ecstatic. He said, "When Ozzy came back it was great. We said, 'let's bury all the past, all the bad blood and everything, and start again.'"[4]

In addition to a number of Black Sabbath classics, the *Reunion* CD, released in October 1998, contained a special treat for fans: the first new Black Sabbath songs featuring Osbourne in twenty years. The songs, "Psycho Man" and "Selling My Soul," were solid numbers that recalled early Sabbath yet had a modern sound. The band's rendition of "Iron Man" on *Reunion* earned the group its first Grammy Award in 2000.

The reunited Black Sabbath embarked on a full-scale tour of European festivals in 1998 and American arenas in 1999. The band would also headline the Ozzfests in 1999, 2001, 2004, and 2005. At the same time, the band members continued their solo careers, deciding they would rather concentrate on their own work than record a new Black Sabbath album.

Osbourne released the album *Down to Earth* in 2001, while Iommi released his first solo album in 2000. Titled *Iommi,* the album featured a supporting cast of well-known musicians, including Dave Grohl of Nirvana and the Foo

Fighters, Billy Corgan of Smashing Pumpkins, Billy Idol, and, on one track, Osbourne.

Iommi said, "I enjoyed the experience of working with a lot of people because I'd never done it before. It's something different for me. I've always done the thing [Black Sabbath] that people expected."[5]

Butler, who had recorded his first solo album, *Plastic Planet,* in 1995, also released *Black Science* in 1997 and *Ohmwork* in 2005.

Though Black Sabbath did not record a new album, several compilation CDs were released. These included a two-disc greatest hits album chronicling the Osbourne years titled *Symptom of the Universe* and a two-disc live album, *Past Lives,* both released in 2002. *Black Box,* which included all eight of the Osbourne-era CDs, was released in 2004, and a single-disc Osbourne years collection titled *Greatest Hits 1970–1978* came out in 2006.

In 2007, another version of Black Sabbath reunited. This time it was the return of the Dio-Iommi-Butler-Appice lineup. The reformation began when Rhino Records, which was putting together a Dio-era Black Sabbath greatest hits compilation, asked the band to record two new songs for the CD as a bonus for fans.

Though this lineup had already experienced bad breakups in 1982 and 1992, Dio agreed to fly to London to write the new songs with Iommi. Dio said he adopted the attitude that it was

best to leave the past behind and move forward: "I haven't spoken to them about [the past] at all. You have to reconcile it within yourself, which is what I've done. I'm not going to let what happened sour my memories. I never thought we would do this again, but I've always liked the guys."[6]

The sessions went so well that Dio and Iommi ended up writing three songs for the album: "Shadow of the Wind," "Ear in the Wall," and "The Devil Cried."

Based on this positive experience, the Dio-fronted Black Sabbath decided to tour to support the album, which was called *Black Sabbath: The Dio Years* and released in April 2007. The band also decided to call itself Heaven and Hell rather than Black Sabbath to avoid confusing fans as to which lineup of Black Sabbath was touring.

Dio understood the reason for the name change but also said that most fans would see the band as Black Sabbath: "My attitude is you could call us Beetle Bailey and the Boys and people are still going to say, 'Sabbath is playing tonight.' I'd like this to work and I think it works under these circumstances. We're playing for the generation of Sabbath fans who started with the *Heaven and Hell* album."[7]

Fans welcomed the Dio-fronted Black Sabbath back with open arms. A sold-out concert at Radio City Music Hall in New York City was recorded for a live CD and DVD. The album and DVD, both titled *Live from Radio City Music Hall,* were released in August 2007. The band continued to tour in 2008.

IN 2007, RONNIE JAMES DIO (RIGHT) AND GEEZER BUTLER (LEFT) PERFORMED AS HEAVEN AND HELL.

In 2009, Heaven and Hell released the Dio-Iommi-Butler-Appice's lineup's first new studio album in seventeen years. The album, titled *The Devil You Know,* was released in April on Rhino Records.

The members of the original Black Sabbath have not ruled out performing again or recording a new album in the future, but for now the band is on hiatus. Iommi said, "There is a possibility. I'd just rather think that when we're ready to do that, we will. We'd love to do it, but until that happens, we stand to [do] whatever else we're going to be doing."[8]

Butler said that a new album with the original lineup would have to have high standards: "We're not going to rush the album because if it doesn't sound right, we won't put it out."[9] Osbourne concurred, stating that if the band did start writing songs, "We all decided if it's not as good as it was in the old days, then we wouldn't do it."[10]

Butler also stated that whether the original lineup works together again is "irrelevant to me. I'm glad we finished on a high note, and I am satisfied with that."[11]

Similarly, Iommi is content with the original lineup's musical legacy. He said, "We've been there for a long time, we've stuck to it, what we believe in. . . . But it's nice to be remembered, and I think things like the Hall of Fame are making sure we're there and will be remembered."[12]

Osbourne continues to work on his solo material and does not seem to mind that the Dio-fronted version of Black Sabbath recorded again. After all the turbulent times the band has experienced in its more than forty-year history, Osbourne is content that the original lineup, even if it never records again, will have ended on a positive note: "If we never do anything more than this, we're friends and we can pick up the phone and say, 'how are you doing,' which is more valuable to me than anything, back to being friends again."[13]

8 IRON MEN

Whether the original Black Sabbath ever plays together again or not, they have achieved an indelible impact on rock and roll and heavy metal music. Both Black Sabbath's music and their aggressive, rebellious nature have inspired and influenced countless bands in a number of rock genres, from hard rock and heavy metal to punk to rap.

Metallica singer and guitarist James Hetfield said he was drawn to Black Sabbath because they challenged the sound and message of popular music. Hetfield said, "Sabbath was everything that the Sixties weren't. Their music was so cool because it was completely anti-hippie."[1]

Green Day singer-guitarist Billie Joe Armstrong said Black Sabbath "would always be the standard for every alienated . . . kid."[2]

The famous rock-and-roll critic Lester Bangs described Black Sabbath's lyrics as "trying to deal with a serious situation in an honest way" and compared the band's song-writing approach to that of the legendary folk musician Bob Dylan. Bangs stated that Sabbath "are a band with a conscience who have looked around them and taken it upon themselves to reflect the chaos in ways they see as positive."[3]

As much as their lyrics have appealed to young people

HARD ROCK BAND LACUNA COIL PERFORMS DURING OZZFEST IN 2006. OZZFEST HIGHLIGHTED UNKNOWN AND KNOWN BANDS.

around the world, Black Sabbath's revolutionary sound was most responsible for its widespread popularity. The band's loud, aggressive, heavy sound and ominous riffs were like nothing that had been heard before, and the band easily stood out from popular blues-based rock bands of the day such as the Who, Cream, and Led Zeppelin.

It was not a coincidence that the band stood out from their peers. Black Sabbath wanted to be different. Butler said, "The reason we got together and made our music in the first place was because nobody else was doing it."[4]

Metallica drummer Lars Ulrich described Black Sabbath's groundbreaking music this way: "They took pre-existing elements of blues, rock and soul, threw in the right amount

FANS ARE A BIG PART OF OZZFEST'S SUCCESS. THESE FANS GATHERED FOR THE 2007 OZZFEST IN MASSACHUSETTS.

of darkness, and fused those elements with a previously undiscovered 'X' factor . . . creating something unheard, unexperienced, unique and utterly groundbreaking with their huge hymns of doom."[5]

Part of the band's appeal was its simplicity. Black Sabbath was more concerned about writing good songs that made an impact rather than worrying about how complex they were or what music critics would think. Ozzy Osbourne said, "The reason we appeal to so many people so instantly is because our sound is good and basic. It doesn't take a lot of understanding. The impact is right there."[6]

Black Sabbath's influence is not limited to heavy metal and hard rock. The rap group Cyprus Hill sampled a part of the song "Black Sabbath" in its own work and the Swedish pop band the Cardigans released their own take on "Iron Man." Be it rock, pop, or rap, Black Sabbath's influence on music over the past forty years is undeniable, and continues today with newer heavy rock bands such as Slipknot and Disturbed citing Sabbath as a major influence.

Judas Priest singer Rob Halford, a heavy metal legend in his own right, summed it up best. Halford said, "I think it's kind of agreed that metal all started with Sabbath. They were a major inspiration to countless new artists. Even today all the new bands on the block cite this great band Sabbath as a major influence."[7]

TIMELINE

1948—Tony Iommi born February 19; Bill Ward born May 5; Ozzy Osbourne born December 3.

1949—Geezer Butler born July 17.

1968—Iommi and Ward play together in Mythology; Butler performs in Rare Breed; Osbourne places ad in record shop that reads, "Ozzy Zig Requires Gig"; Butler approaches Osbourne to join Rare Breed, but band breaks up before Osbourne can audition; Iommi and Ward answer Osbourne's ad after Mythology breaks up; Iommi, Osbourne, Ward, and Butler form the Polka Tulk Blues Band; name shortened to Polka Tulk.

1969—Band changes name to Earth; writes song "Black Sabbath" and changes band name to Black Sabbath.

1970—Debut album *Black Sabbath* released February 13; second album *Paranoid* released September 18, hits number one on British charts, reaches number twelve in the United States; band performs first show in the United States October 30, in Glassboro, New Jersey.

1972—*Volume IV,* first album recorded in the United States, released September 25.

1973—*Sabbath Bloody Sabbath,* recorded in Clearwell Castle in southwest England near Wales, released December 1; reaches number four on British charts and number eleven in the United States.

1974—Band tours Europe and America, plays the California Jam Festival before two hundred thousand people.

1975—Band begins to show frustration, tension, and exhaustion due to years of drug and alcohol abuse, financial problems, and nonstop recording and touring schedule.

1977—Osbourne leaves band in November, citing personal problems and exhaustion; Sabbath recruits singer Dave Walker of Savoy Brown to replace Osbourne; band begins writing next album with Walker.

1978—Osbourne returns in January; band records its eighth album, *Never Say Die!,* in Toronto; December 11 concert in Albuquerque, New Mexico, is original lineup's last show for seven years.

1979—Band fires Osbourne, replaces him with American singer Ronnie James Dio.

1980—Black Sabbath, with Ronnie James Dio singing, releases *Heaven and Hell* in April; Ward leaves band during *Heaven and Hell* tour, replaced by Vinny Appice.

1982—Dio and Appice leave Black Sabbath and are replaced by former Deep Purple singer Ian Gillan and Ward.

1985—Original lineup reunites for three-song set at Live Aid benefit concert in Philadelphia.

1986—*Seventh Star* is released with former Deep Purple bassist-singer Glenn Hughes on vocals.

1992—Iommi-Butler-Dio-Appice lineup reunites, releases *Dehumanizer;* Butler, Ward, and Iommi perform four songs with Osbourne during an Osbourne concert in California.

1997—Osbourne, Iommi, and Butler reunite during Ozzfest, Osbourne drummer Mike Bordin fills in for Ward; Ward returns for two reunion shows in December at the Birmingham National Exhibition Centre.

1998—*Reunion* live album is released, featuring performances from 1997 Birmingham concerts plus two new songs; original lineup tours Europe; former drummer Cozy Powell dies in automobile accident.

1999—Original lineup tours the United States, headlines Ozzfest.

2000—Band wins Grammy Award for Best Metal Performance for live version of "Iron Man" from *Reunion.*

2001—Band headlines Ozzfest.

2004—Band headlines Ozzfest; *Black Box: The Complete Original Black Sabbath (1970–1978)* is released, which includes all eight studio albums with Osbourne and a DVD of early performance footage.

2005—Band headlines Ozzfest.

2006—Original lineup inducted into Rock and Roll Hall of Fame.

2007—A greatest hits album, *Black Sabbath: The Dio Years,* is released, featuring three new songs from the Dio-Iommi-Butler-Appice lineup; band tours under the name Heaven and Hell to avoid

confusion with Osbourne-fronted lineup;
Heaven and Hell releases *Live at Radio City
Music Hall* CD and DVD.

2008—*The Rules of Hell* five-CD box set featuring
remastered versions of Dio-era albums is
released.

2009—Heaven and Hell release new studio album,
The Devil You Know.

2010—Ronnie James Dio dies after a long battle with
cancer on May 16.

BAND MEMBERS

Singers

Ozzy Osbourne, 1969–1978, 1997–2007

Ronnie James Dio (Dio, Rainbow), 1979–1982, 1992, 2007–2010

Ian Gillan (Deep Purple), 1983–1984

David Donato, 1984–1985

Glenn Hughes (Deep Purple), 1985–1986

Ray Gillen (Badlands), 1986–1987

Tony Martin, 1987–1991, 1993–1995

Rob Halford (Judas Priest), two shows in 1992, one show in 2004

Guitarists

Tony Iommi, 1969–present

Bass Guitarists

Geezer Butler, 1969–1984, 1990–1994, 1997–present

Dave Spitz, 1985–1986, 1987

Bob Daisley (Ozzy Osbourne band), 1986

Jo Burt, 1987

Laurence Cottle, 1988

Neil Murray (Whitesnake), 1989–1991, 1994–1995

Drummers

Bill Ward, 1969–1980, 1982–1983, 1984–1985, 1994, 1997–2007

Vinny Appice (Dio), 1980–1982, 1992, 1998, 2007–present

Bev Bevan (Blue Oyster Cult) 1983–1984, 1987

Eric Singer (Kiss, Alice Cooper, Badlands), 1985–1987

Terry Chimes (The Clash), 1987–1988

Cozy Powell (Rainbow, the Jeff Beck Group), 1994–1995

Bobby Rondinelli (Rainbow, Quiet Riot, Blue Oyster Cult), 1995

Mike Bordin (Ozzy Osbourne band, Faith No More), 1997

Keyboardists (Non-official members)

Geoff Nicholls, 1979–2004

Adam Wakeman, 2004–2006

Scott Warren, 2007–present

DISCOGRAPHY

1970 *Black Sabbath*

Paranoid

1971 *Master of Reality*

1972 *Volume IV*

1973 *Sabbath Bloody Sabbath*

1975 *Sabotage*

1976 *We Sold Our Soul for Rock 'N' Roll*

Technical Ecstasy

1978 *Never Say Die!*

1980 *Live at Last*

Heaven and Hell

1981 *Mob Rules*

1982 *Live Evil*

1983 *Born Again*

1986 *Seventh Star*

1987 *The Eternal Idol*

1989 *Headless Cross*

1990 *Tyr*

1992 *Dehumanizer*

1994 *Cross Purposes*

1995 *Cross Purposes Live*

Forbidden

1998 *Reunion*

2002 *Past Lives*

Symptom of the Universe: The Original Black Sabbath 1970–1978

2004 *Black Box: The Complete Original Black Sabbath (1970–1978)*

2006 *Greatest Hits 1970–1978*

2007 *Black Sabbath: The Dio Years*

Black Sabbath: Live at Hammersmith Odeon

Heaven and Hell: Live at Radio City Music Hall

2008 *The Rules of Hell*

2009 *Heaven and Hell: The Devil You Know*

CONCERT TOURS[1]

1970 Black Sabbath Tour

1970–1971 Paranoid Tour

1971–1972 Master of Reality Tour

1972–1973 Volume IV Tour

1974 Sabbath Bloody Sabbath Tour

1975 Sabotage Tour

1976–1977 Technical Ecstasy Tour

1978 Ten-Year Anniversary Tour

1980 Heaven and Hell Tour

1981 Mob Rules Tour

1983 Born Again Tour

1986 Seventh Star Tour

1987 Eternal Idol Tour

1989 Headless Cross Tour

1990 Tyr Tour

1992 Dehumanizer Tour

1994 Cross Purposes Tour

1995 Forbidden Tour

1997 Ozzfest '97, two U.K. reunion shows

1998 Reunion Tour (Europe only), Ozzfest U.K. (one date)

1999 Reunion Tour, Ozzfest '99

2001 Ozzfest 2001

2004 Ozzfest 2004

2005 Ozzfest 2005

2007 Heaven and Hell Tour

2008 Metal Masters Tour (Heaven and Hell)

2009 Heaven and Hell Tour

GLOSSARY

12-bar blues—A song based on a series of basic chord progressions. Beginning bands often play 12-bar blues songs.

apprentice—A person training to learn a specific job or skill.

chord—On the guitar, a combination of three or more musical notes played simultaneously.

flower power—A phrase associated with the hippie and peace movements of the late 1960s.

geezer—British slang meaning a cool person. The equivalent of "cool dude" in American slang.

hippie—A person who advocates for peace and rejects what he or she considers the standards of mainstream society. In the 1960s, hippies wore casual, folksy clothing, kept their hair long, and staged large anti-war and social justice protests.

progressive rock—A style of rock music known for its complicated musical arrangements and the technical skill of its musicians.

riff—A short, often repeated, rhythmic musical phrase. Heavy metal music is known for its guitar riffs.

row house—One in a row of houses in an urban setting having the same design.

Sabbath—A day of rest and religious observance; observed by Jews on Saturday and Christians on Sunday.

sabotage—The act of trying to hurt, interfere with, or weaken another person.

sheet metal—Metal formed into thin and flat pieces that can be cut and bent into a variety of different shapes.

soldering iron—A rod-shaped tool with a pointed tip that uses heat to attach metal parts to one another.

subpoena—A written document directing a person to appear in court.

Woodstock—Famous hippie music festival held from August 15–18, 1969, on a farm in New York State.

CHAPTER NOTES

Chapter 1. Heavy Metal Hall of Famers

1. "Rock and Roll Hall of Fame Induction Speech," *Billboard.com,* March 15, 2006, <http://www.billboard.com/news/archives/2006/03/hof_induction_speech.html> (February 15, 2008).
2. Mike Stark, *Black Sabbath: An Oral History*, ed. Dave Marsh (New York: HarperCollins, 1998), p. 104.
3. "Full Text of Metallica's Black Sabbath Induction Speech Available," *Roadrunner Records,* March 15, 2006, <http://www.roadrunnerrecords.com/blabbermouth.net/news.aspx?mode=Article&newsitemID=49600> (February 15, 2008).
4. Brian Aberback, "Sabbath's Iommi Makes Solo Debut," *The Record,* October 17, 2000, p. Y01.

Chapter 2. Meet the Band

1. Mick Wall, *Ozzy Osbourne: Diary of a Madman* (London: Zomba Books, 1985), p. 11.
2. Joel McIver, *Sabbath Bloody Sabbath* (London: Omnibus Press, 2007), p. 7.
3. Ibid., p. 9.
4. Carol Clerk, *Ozzy Osbourne: Diary of a Madman:*

The Stories Behind the Songs (New York: Thunder Mouth Press, 2002), p. 10.

5. McIver, p. 9.

6. Wall, p. 17.

7. Ibid., p. 18.

8. McIver, p. 12.

9. Wall, p. 18.

10. McIver, p. 16.

11. Ibid., p. 8.

12. Martin Popoff, *Black Sabbath: Doom Let Loose* (Toronto: ECW Press, 2006), p. 4.

13. McIver, p. 8.

14. Chris Gill, "Tony Iommi Holiday Issue Cover Story Preview," *Guitar World,* n.d., <http://www.guitarworld.com/article/tony_iommi_december_cover_story_preview?page=0%2C1> (November 25, 2008).

15. McIver, p. 12.

16. Ibid., p. 14.

17. Popoff, p. 4.

18. McIver, p. 14.

19. Ibid., p. 18.

20. Ibid., p. 6.

21. Popoff, p. 7.

22. Ibid., p. 8.

23. Ibid., p. 7.

24. McIver, p. 11.

25. Ibid.

Chapter 3. From Birmingham to the Big Time

1. David Konow, *Bang Your Head: The Rise and Fall of Heavy Metal* (New York: Three Rivers Press, 2002), p. 3.
2. Mick Wall, *Ozzy Osbourne: Diary of a Madman* (London: Zomba Books, 1985), p. 23.
3. Joel McIver, *Sabbath Bloody Sabbath* (London: Omnibus Press, 2007), p. 78.
4. Ibid., p. 20.
5. Ibid.
6. Ibid.
7. Ibid., p. 21.
8. Ibid., p. 25.
9. Ibid., p. 24.
10. Ibid.
11. *Don't Blame Me: The Tales of Ozzy Osbourne*, DVD, directed by Jeb Brien (Sony, 1991).
12. Chris Welch, "Lords of This World," essay from the booklet accompanying, *Black Box: The Complete Original Black Sabbath (1970–1978)* box set, Rhino Records, 2004, p. 5.
13. Ibid.
14. Martin Popoff, *Black Sabbath: Doom Let Loose* (Toronto: ECW Press, 2006), p. 11.
15. *Don't Blame Me: The Tales of Ozzy Osbourne.*
16. Popoff, p. 12.
17. Wall, p. 24.

18. McIver, p. 38.

19. Ibid.

20. Wall, p. 28.

21. Welch, p. 6.

22. Popoff, pp. 34–35.

23. Ibid., pp. 35–36.

24. Robin Green, "How Black Was My Sabbath,"
    Rolling Stone, October 28, 1971, <http://www.
    rollingstone.com/artists/blacksabbath/articles/
    story/9437616/how_black_was_my_sabbath>
    (January 31, 2009).

25. Brian Ives, "A Hard Road," essay from the booklet
    accompanying *Black Box: The Complete Original
    Black Sabbath (1970–1978)* box set (Rhino
    Records, 2004), p. 32.

26. Carol Clerk, *Ozzy Osbourne: Diary of a Madman:
    The Stories Behind the Songs* (New York:
    Thunder Mouth Press, 2002), p. 32.

27. McIver, p. 29.

28. Brian Aberback, "Sabbath's Iommi Makes Solo
    Debut," *The Record,* October 17, 2000, p. Y01.

29. Popoff, p. 70.

30. Ibid., p. 71.

31. McIver, p. 67.

32. Popoff, p. 84.

33. McIver, p. 74.

34. Popoff, p. 87.

35. Ibid.

36. Clerk, p. 48.

37. Popoff, p. 87.

38. Ibid., p. 90.

39. Gordon Fletcher, "Sabbath Bloody Sabbath," *Rolling Stone,* February 14, 1974, <http://www. rollingstone.com/artists/blacksabbath/albums/ album/227113/review/5946174/sabbath_bloody_ sabbath> (February 3, 2009).

Chapter 4. A Hard Road

1. Brian Ives, "A Hard Road," essay from the booklet accompanying *Black Box: The Complete Original Black Sabbath (1970–1978)* box set (Rhino Records, 2004), p. 36.

2. Ibid., pp. 34–35.

3. *Black Sabbath—The Last Supper,* DVD, directed by Jeb Brien (Sony, 1999).

4. Ives, p. 27.

5. Interview portion of *The Ozzman Cometh* CD (Epic, 1997).

6. Chris Ingham, *The Book of Metal: The Most Comprehensive Encyclopedia of Metal Music Ever Created* (New York: Thunder Mouth Press, 2002), p. 28.

7. Mick Wall, *Ozzy Osbourne: Diary Of A Madman* (London: Zomba Books, 1985), p. 50.

8. Joel McIver, *Sabbath Bloody Sabbath* (London: Omnibus Press, 2007), p. 94.

9. Ibid., p. 93.

10. Martin Popoff, *Black Sabbath: Doom Let Loose* (Toronto: ECW Press, 2006), p. 128.

11. Wall, p. 63.

12. Ibid., p. 64.

13. Ibid., p. 58.

14. Popoff, p. 143.

15. Wall, p. 64.

16. Popoff, p. 158.

17. Ibid., p. 160.

18. *Black Sabbath—The Last Supper.*

19. Ibid.

20. Mike Stark, *Black Sabbath: An Oral History,* ed. Dave Marsh (New York: HarperCollins, 1998), p. 38.

21. Ibid.

22. Carol Clerk, *Ozzy Osbourne: Diary of a Madman: The Stories Behind the Songs* (New York: Thunder Mouth Press, 2002), p. 65.

Chapter 5. Never Say Die

1. Joel McIver, *Sabbath Bloody Sabbath* (London: Omnibus Press, 2007), p. 124.

2. Martin Popoff, *Black Sabbath: Doom Let Loose* (Toronto: ECW Press, 2006), p. 162.

3. Mike Stark, *Black Sabbath: An Oral History,* ed. Dave Marsh (New York: HarperCollins, 1998), p. 50.

4. Popoff, p. 160

5. Ibid., p. 159.

6. *Black Sabbath—The Last Supper,* DVD, directed by Jeb Brien (Sony, 1999).

7. Jerry McCulley, "The Roots of Spinal Tap," *Gibson. com,* May 23, 2008, <http://www.gibson.com/en-us/ Lifestyle/Features/therootsofspinaltapwith/> (June 7, 2009).

8. Stark, p. 31.

Chapter 6. *Blizzard of Ozz*

1. Joel McIver, *Sabbath Bloody Sabbath* (London: Omnibus Press, 2007), p. 109.

2. *Black Sabbath—The Last Supper,* DVD, directed by Jeb Brien (Sony, 1999).

3. David Konow, *Bang Your Head: The Rise and Fall of Heavy Metal* (New York: Three Rivers Press, 2002), p. 117.

4. Christina Titus, "Hall of Fame Focus: Black Sabbath," *Billboard.com,* n.d., <http://www. billboard.com/bbcom/rockhall/2006/feature/ bsabbath.01.jsp> (April 15, 2008).

5. McIver, p. 333.

Chapter 7. Reunited

1. Mick Wall, *Ozzy Osbourne: Diary Of A Madman* (London: Zomba Books, 1985), p. 167.

2. Martin Popoff, *Black Sabbath: Doom Let Loose* (Toronto: ECW Press, 2006), p. 282.

3. Martin Popoff, *20th Century Rock and Roll:*

Heavy Metal (Toronto: Collector's Guide Publishing, 2000), p. 13.

4. Joel McIver, *Sabbath Bloody Sabbath* (London: Omnibus Press, 2007), p. 274.

5. Brian Aberback, "Sabbath's Iommi Makes Solo Debut," *The Record,* October 17, 2000, p. Y01.

6. Brian Aberback, "Dio Back in the Mix," *The Record,* March 23, 2007, p. G15.

7. Ibid.

8. McIver, p. 276.

9. Popoff, *Doom Let Loose,* p. 333.

10. Brian Ives, "A Hard Road," essay from the booklet accompanying *Black Box: The Complete Original Black Sabbath (1970–1978)* box set, (Rhino Records, 2004), p. 41.

11. Ibid.

12. McIver, p. 375.

13. *Black Sabbath—The Last Supper,* DVD, directed by Jeb Brien (Sony, 1999).

Chapter 8. Iron Men

1. Carol Clerk, *Ozzy Osbourne: Diary of a Madman: The Stories Behind the Songs* (New York: Thunder Mouth Press, 2002), p. 52.

2. Chris Welch, "Lords of This World," essay from the booklet accompanying *Black Box: The Complete Original Black Sabbath (1970–1978)* box set (Rhino Records, 2004), p. 2.

3. David Konow, *Bang Your Head: The Rise and Fall of Heavy Metal* (New York: Three Rivers Press, 2002), p. 13.

4. Ibid.

5. "Full Text of Metallica's Black Sabbath Induction Speech Available," *Roadrunner Records,* March 15, 2006, <http://www.roadrunnerrecords.com/blabbermouth.net/news.aspx?mode=Article&newsitemID=49600> (February 15, 2008).

6. Clerk, p. 23.

7. Ian Christie, *Sound of the Beast: The Complete Headbanging History of Heavy Metal* (New York: HarperCollins, 2004), p. 341.

Concert Tours

1. "Tour Dates," *Black Sabbath Online,* n.d., <http://www.black-sabbath.com/tourdates/index.html> (June 1, 2009).

FURTHER READING

Books

Bidini, Dave. *For Those About to Rock: A Road Map for Being in a Band.* Plattsburg, NY: Tundra Books of Northern New York, 2004.

Handyside, Christopher. *Rock.* Chicago, Ill.: Heinemann Library, 2006.

Koopmans, Andy. *The Osbournes.* San Diego, Calif.: Lucent Books, 2003.

Rosen, Steven. *History of Rock.* St. Catharines, Ont.: Crabtree Pub., 2009.

Saucerman, Linda. *Ozzy Osbourne and Kelly Osbourne.* New York: Rosen Publishing Group, 2004.

Spilsbury, Richard. *Should I Play the Guitar?* Chicago, Ill.: Heinemann Library, 2007.

Internet Addresses

Black Sabbath online
<http://www.black-sabbath.com/>

Heaven and Hell
<http://heavenandhelllive.com/>

INDEX